The

Research

Sector:

-Towards A Social Policy & Political Economy of The Future

By Alan Peter Garfoot Jnr. Cert. H.E.

The Research Sector:

-Towards A Social Policy & Political Economy of The Future

By: Alan Peter Garfoot Jnr. Cert. H.E.

ISBN: 978-1-4717-2435-0

18/04/2022

The New World Thought Disorder:

London.

Contents

Abstract:

Through investing in government funded research, to establish public owned patents in new areas of technological development and scientific inquiry, the wealth of an individual nation can prosper, as these goods cannot be mass produced by other countries cheaper. This, in a global environment ensures the economic prosperity, political sovereignty, educational freedom, flourishing of the job market and value of exports; the research directed economy is a blueprint for how to run the county at a profit for the people, not a loss.`

This thesis presents a left-wing socialism based perspective and also separately as a right-wing political ideology and social policy as well as humanism based Neo-Modernism can be adapted easily to either style of state apparatus. The rest of this article will therefore consist of an investigation into the nature of humanism as a sociopolitical doctrine of progress and how neomodernism is a potential future embodiment of positive human ideals deeply rooted in humanism only reinvented in a new more evolved form

Introduction:

We live in a world where the existential liberalism of positive cultural individualism has corrupted into a selfish egotistical embitterment against the poor, weak and marginalised. We are hoodwinked into stifling others whilst claiming superiority, through believing in the stigma and stereotypes, made popular through the hegemonic mass media who only represent the opinions and ideals of the sociopolitical kleptoratic elite they represent, (Gramsci, 2005). This is as the mass repetition of the novel, original and unique forever fades the true value of the applied capacities of human ingenuity, potential and talent away into an ambient ideological background stagnation of the intellectual and creative apathy of a generation which fails to understand itself and struggles to be original, (Adorno, 2001).

An ideologically pragmatic cultural dystopia where no-one in society believes that they have the personal capacities let alone can even dream of achieving the sociocultural ideals or values of personal achievement, social mobility or cultural progress. Where the mass media propagation of dominant economic beliefs and established political ideologies into the sociocultural meme-pool dynamic of societies constantly evolving ideological perspective controls us through cultural conditioning and socialisation into our 'habitus' of beliefs, (Bourdieau, 1977). We are collectively subdued into believing the popularised opinions of whatever current 'moral panic' serves either the mass media economic or dominant social groups political or ideological interests the most, through sensitisation, repetition and over-reporting, (Cohen, 1972).

We are set in perpetual ideological conflict against each other as people and groups, against our better judgement as intellectuals and thinkers, and against our interests both as existential individuals and agents of social change and progress, (Marx, 1832; Marx, 1848). Because of this our state of cultural consciousness never advances or evolves to the level where we are able to see our collective social interests as shared and are therefore capable of actualising our true individual potential inside us or achieving the real social progress our generation is capable of, (Maslow, 1943).

In this manuscript we see a resurrection of the ideology of humanism; and the enlightenment cultural ideals of the belief in science and scientific progress; the belief in the capacity of science to positively influence human destiny and change the world for the better, (Comte, 1865). It is with this I begin the creation of a stir of new ideology in the social and cultural sciences and out into the greater spectrum of the academic humanities as a whole, in order to to shed some light upon our path into the future and our collective human social destiny. These are the main topics I shall consider as especially relevant to this discussion: The first topic I discuss is the fundamental nature of humanism as a part of the positivist enlightenment culture of science. I shall be assessing it as an agent of personal development, social progress and an instigator of 'the memetic evolution of cultural space' within society, (Garfoot, 2010). I shall also be expanding our conceptual understanding of humanism as an academic ideology of positivism through considering the capacities and potentials of human creative nature alongside the already established sciences of human rational nature as an active psychological agent of personal evolution, cultural change, and social progress. (Mill, 1859)

I shall consider the concepts ideological value within the ethnocentrism of the subculture of scientific ideology which considers the achievement of social progress, cultural evolution and scientific advancement as three of the most pinnacle concerns of intellectual activity. That the fruition of all three can be considered as true ethical ideals worth striving for, believing in and constitutes a true candidate for good positive existentialist faith (Sartre, 1948).

Then having fully cemented my sociocultural perspective in humanism I shall form in the section titled critical analysis pull together and form what is a political scientist and social ideologist and academic intellectuals answer to the current most fundamental sociopolitical crisis of our time: Hyper-capitalism. A solution in terms of cultural ideology, social policy and political economy to the impending economic downwards spiral of the international Debt Fuelled Economy (DFE) and suggest an alternative to the capitalist self-fulfilling prophecy of global wealth polarisation and social inequality (Willis, 1977; Becker, 1963; Merton, 1968).

I shall look at what I call the research based model of global economic social interaction and functioning, as a way out of of the International Monitory Fund (IMF) national deficit debt fuelled economy as a way for national economies to regain their political and economic strength and sovereignty. I shall also look at the Research Based Economy (RBE) as a solution to undergraduate higher education funding, decline in the job market and the negative

7

aspects of globalisation and mass production that threaten to cause an imbalance of economic strength in the export market in the near and far future.

Finally in this academic dissertation I shall look at the potential of the ideology of humanism and of the Positivist enlightenment era intellectual ideals of the meta-narratives to undergo the analysis of historical materialism. To see if, as Marx predicted, there eventually exist a form of Neo-Modern revival of left wing political beliefs and ideas which embody all the positive ideals and social aspects of currently existing international sociopolitical structures and cultures out of which by 'the philosophers of the future' new cultural ideology will start to form, (Nietzsche, 1886)

To conclude I shall consider liberal democratic ideology, free higher education, individual human civil rights, freedom of speech and freedom from oppression as pivotal in the creation of true egalitarian cultural consciousness on any kind of true social level. This is done through creating positive empowering creative 'cultural space' for all individuals to express, learn, grow and evolve, to create the right social and cultural conditions for the bud of the perfect future society to grow in the soil of the present in the realisation of the idealist vision of creating the utopian green society before the Human race can start realistically considering interplanetary or interstellar colonisation, (Garfoot, 2012).

Theoretical Background:

This piece of new theoretical synthesis and intellectual development is a fresh wedge of sociocultural refinement, designed to cut straight through the intellectual and creative cultural decadence and sociopolitical stagnation of the modern day. As we try to overcome the decay of the postmodern cultural vacuum, of the under-actualised existential potential that all individuals have, which has been left to fall into ruin by the process of the emotive enslavement, of our intellectual autonomy, to the hype of the latest 'moral panic' that the mass media sensitises us to (Cohen, 1972).

Embodied in our enabled capacities of metacognition, engendered by the humanist belief in our innate human right to our social freedoms; we see the idealist liberal democratic hope for the achievement of social progress born into its existential reality. (Metcalfe & Shimamura, 1994) I believe it is through breaking away from all religious prerequisites for morality, striving for the right to develop our personal ethical autonomy and championing the collective betterment of the human condition for all we see the humanist social and ethical ideal really define itself.

With its philosophical foundations in the classical roots of Aristotelian virtue ethics and the Deontological categorical imperative of Immanuel Kant, we see the intellectual basis for all humanistic ethical consideration take its true ideological shape and form. (Aristotle, 2002; Kant, 1762; Kant, 1790) That through placing belief in the rationally achieved emotional temperament, thoughts and consequent behaviours of human individuals as opposed to the innate natural

9

divinity of higher powers, indoctrinated scripture and dominant religious authorities as the central basis of ethical consideration the true intellectual and cultural enablement of human autonomy emerge.

But before social progress can be achieved as a collective cultural actualisation, its methodological form must first be rationally schematised, as both humanist and neomodernist cross-cultural political ideology and international economic policy. With a fusion of new intellectual ideas and subsequent ideological ideals we see form out of a collective sociocultural meta-analysis of relevant theoretical deductions and their inferred conceptual alignments the rebirth of the humanist social ideal and ethical paradigm.

A paradigm of social idealism whose causation is the connective glue between current and future perspectives of cultural understanding, political policy and economic operation; each within its own unique sphere of pragmatically arrived at locality of meaning, truth and operation. So forming out of the deconstructed conceptual quanta and theoretical qualia of the current incomplete and fragmented old political, social and economic whole a new unified central ideological core of metaphysical objectivity within the intellectual culture of the humanities and social sciences.

The creation of an anthropological order of scientific objectivity, formed of a central ethnocentric unifying core created out of the cultural relativism of meanings through progressive ideological synthesis. An cultural core of scientific objectivity surrounded by a panopticon of an intersubjectively blended spectral colour gradients as representing the different fundamentally innate existential meanings representative of the expression and experience of human thought, emotion, nature, mind and culture.

When we combine the human faculty of intellectual reason gained through analysis and the unique capacities that we have for creativity and imagination, we engender our potential for synthesis. When these two intellectual powers are combined together in an attempt to create a new theory of explanation out of our previous understandings we see the progressive ideals of the old social system being reborn in the future epoch to come.

For instance, based upon this, the Marxists believe in the historical materialism or scientific law-like predictability of social destiny. The causation, origin, truth, nature and ultimate successive progression of our self creating fate and the destiny of our social system. The achievement of the intellectual enlightenment, emotional emancipation and empathic connectedness of collective cultural consciousness.

Where the individual members of human society and civilisation are empowered to a positive destiny of actualisation. This is one such idea upon the neomodern progression of humanist social democracy and the intrinsic value of the ideal of personal liberty. This could also be said to be equally true of neomodern humanism in its attempts to unite under a positive global banner of a planet unified on a global scale through enlightened understanding, empathy and respect.

With the aim of eliminating inequalities, stigma and ignorance from our opinions and beliefs through evolving the perspective we have, so we are better informed and autonomous in our decisions. We do this through creating the ideal conditions for economic prosperity, individual freedom, international power sharing and a universal belief in personal flourishing through having dignity and human rights.

But it is true it could be said that both our behaviour and our cycles of thought appear to be following a pattern of logical causation and therefore could be believed to be a scientifically predictable system in its fundamental nature. So too could be said of the futures progressive realisation of cultural ideals, their emotive energies and the intellectual refinement and creative elaboration of the innate unique concept into the mass-produced mundane replication of it as physical objects, (Adorno, 2001).

The positively autonomous individual seeks the further emancipation of our positive higher emotional, intellectual and metaphysical nature through the insight gained from evolving and developing our personal knowledge and understanding. That liberated from the shackles of Plato's existential cave analogy we can strive for, successfully achieve and realise the modern-day Humanist ambitions for collective social progress and the Aristotelian philosophical ideal of the 'eudiomonia' of a flourishing human race.

That together we should work towards the improvement of the existential realities and social conditions of all individuals who along with ourselves bear the burden of some aspect of the inequality of the human condition or in some way are forced to endure unnecessary suffering or undue oppression in their 'lifeworld', (Mead, 1967). We seek an enlightenment which inspires our unique interpretation of our collective cultural understandings, both of ourselves, each other and the meaning we give to our reality.

We aspire to the creation of to a new Neo-Modern zenith of the realised and actualized scientific, creative, intellectual, cultural, social, personal and technological knowledge, abilities and capacities that we as the human race have developed so far. We desire an accurate and sound scientifically objective comprehension of both the nature of reality and the meaning of life.

Pragmatically developing a personal belief system, which is both intellectually enlightened and pragmatically enabling, which engenders the development of personal autonomy and agency. So as that together, through the introspective realisation of our collective 'cultural consciousness' we can each reclaim our freedom from what in his day was religion but which is now the clutches of the current day mass-media enslavement, (Marx, 1832; Marx, 1848).

A socialised and conditioned reactionary predisposition toward ideological stagnation and ignorance through the emotive over-reporting through the emotive hype of subjective yet prevalent opinions reinforcing an overconfidence in unverified or justified beliefs. This is a part of the great cultural challenge of 'self-overcoming' of the free thinking individuals of our days and times as they create for themselves a future for all which is satisfying, rewarding, truly positive and genuinely worth living.

Developing further the faith that Humanism holds in the natural faculties that human individuals have of logic and reason, then combining these abilities that we possess naturally as humans within the interpretive frame of reference of our creative capacities for imagination, synthesis and spontaneous autonomous social action. We realise the duality of the intellect and the imagination in the creation of practical cultural wisdom and development of our ethical perspective and behaviour.

I intend to provide the grounds not just for an advancement of human knowledge through reason, but develop it further in its consideration into the form of its ideal state as the wisdom of its practical ethical application. Individually achieved through considering the personal interpretations we have of the cultural representations of collective reflection upon the ethical application of the power of knowledge and current capacities of developed science. This dynamic must be considered if we are to be successful in the cultivation of our ideal personal enablement of our autonomy out of the collective cultural representations of the ideological conceptual qualities which determine our civilisations and societies level of ethical capacity and moral responsibility.

It is through considering the cultural development of human creative understanding, into an empathy driven ethical perspective of a real, true, actual and practical wisdom that we are capable of achieving 'cultural consciousness' as the realisation of our true higher nature. This realisation is essential if it is so to guide our application of science and technology to the individual, social, collective, cultural and literal inheritance of the problems and difficulties innate to the intellectual analysis of, and the objective existential reality of; the human condition.

This is due to the fact that as a generation we have inherited the sociocultural, economic, ethical and practical problems of the past from our forefathers, and they themselves from our own more distant ancestors. There is a natural intergenerational passing on of the progressively evolved state of the human condition, and from this the development of our tangent of shared human destiny, one which we as a collection of

14

societies and unity of civilisation pursue throughout our lifetimes.

So, for more than a century now, the enlightenment meta-narrative ideals that science and reason can save humanity from the ravages of nature, and the failings of its own collective existential immaturity and its ensuing state of crisis; lay wrecked and in ruin. The violent destruction of the enlightenment ideals and positivist ethical metanarrative, through the application of science and technology to the destructive ends of genocide, war, social oppression and humanities near perpetual enslavement to the authoritarian tyranny of totalitarian power, (Lyotard, 1984).

It is often said that knowledge is power, but knowledge is only power when it is successfully applied to the practical problems that we as a species, society and civilization, together, as a part of the human condition, suffer. Practical problems, which need solutions, that one day we hope and strive in our endeavours to successfully as a global civilisation find solutions to and eventually as one overcome.

That through the realisation of our true socially rooted empathic cultural consciousness, in the collective achievement of our social ambitions, can actually realise, our aspiration for the ideals of true social progress, which one day, we hope to achieve.

But despite our most inspired virtues and enlightened ideals the harsh and grim realities of human suffering, from the pages of our recent social history like the Holocaust, Rwanda and the perpetual state of international economic and political aggression looms over us.

A system which insists on perpetuating the inequalities between, through the exploitation of, other

15

individuals and nations; through the power polarisation at work in human political, economic and social interaction at all levels. The presence of conflict and war across the world is more than enough evidence that humanity still has far to go if it is to finally achieve as an actual reality the collective betterment of the quality of life of all for whom the human condition is a burden.

But in order to do this we must actualise and objectify all which we are autonomously capable of in order claim our birthright as human beings and achieve what we individually and collectively deserve. It is this realisation of our inner positive human capacities, qualities and nature; and realisation of the humanist ideology within the enlightenment ideals for progress which enshrines our belief in the greater value of humanity.

Finding within ourselves to desire to improve the quality of life of all individuals, the world over, within our inner nature, is both a part of the legacy of our lives and of the living memory of the ancestors. The pursuit of the progressive personal, social and cultural honouration of their legacy of ideals and virtues which guide us in the creation of our future which we make for ourselves as we endeavour to create a better future for ourselves and our children.

Through embodying and objectifying the genuine cultural values and positive human virtues of freedom, equality, peace, love and compassionate empathy as a fundamental part of our social paradigm and code of ethics. An empathy and enlightened culture which strives for greater and better that we should ourselves endeavour to pass on to our children.

As the legacy of our chosen collective social destiny, to shed light upon the path that together we are on, and guide the footsteps which humanity will walk, long after we have succumb to our mortal fate and ceased to be. We must together strive for the cultural empowerment of ourselves and each others individual self and will. Through manifesting the true ideals, moral virtues and values of our individual potential and positive emotional nature that we are all individually, uniquely and innately capable of developing within our achievement of the infinite individuality as human beings.

An individuality achieved through a real, genuine and true faith in ourselves and each other regardless of culture, scripture, religion, lifestyle or experience. Embodied as the empowerment of our individual emotional, intellectual and creative will, enshrined in our collective, cultural and individual social ideals, ethical standards, and culturally defined context and frame of reference. The conceptualisation of a schema of mutual understanding which is universal enough in its intellectual comprehension and cultural interpretation to be accurately translated to all others and realised too ourselves.

A uniqueness that as innately valuable, and is a desirable concept in the formulation of ethical virtue and realised positive nature, that applies to all people, across all nations, cultural boundaries, social realities and individual ideologies. New ideologies and belief structures yet to be truly realised as definitive milestones in the whole history of collective, positive, mutually beneficial human cultural endeavour. Perspectives which should enable and safeguard the realisation and achievement of our emotional emancipation and intellectual enlightenment within our lifetimes.

So far in human history we have all too often seen the ugly brutality of the ego-driven selfish desire for power and the visceral satisfaction of victimising and abusing a minority group. Often done to reinforce the cultural belief that one is innately better or superior to somebody else, in an attempt to justify and legitimise the polarization of the ownership of wealth and power, through making such oppression the ideological core of the kleptocratic or despotic elite.

Engendering through personal privilege, the individual, innate, yet inherently subjective belief in their own superiority. A belief they cling to when confronted by the existential crisis of their relative moral insignificance as the terror of the final moment of life edges ever closer in. When considered in the greater scheme of things we are eclipsed by the sheer scale of a universe. Something which we can barely comprehend in its true nature as actual reality. Something whose magnificence and magnitude dwarfs our own existence by an unfathomable near infinity of stars and galaxies.

This is a call to the resurrection of those highly valued modern and postmodern humanist ideals that perished long ago. Empowerment through a belief not in a higher power which can somehow influence the nature of reality to change the future for us, purely on the grounds of personal favour or special religiously attained personal privilege. But through having good faith in the remarkable and incredible potential which we each contain like a seed within ourselves for the realisation of our true individuality to grow.

Then together flourish through the emancipation of our emotional nature and the realisation of our intellectual enlightenment. Achieving successfully the endeavour of collective social progress. The achievement of new, better and more improved moral perspectives in the form of our universal ideologies symbolic meanings, gained through evolving our cultural standards and ideals.

Then through this transforming the collective social and personal individual realities of the human race. Through the development of an existential faith that we can all, when introspectively equipped, achieve. To see the inner beauty in our nature and find a degree of freedom from our enslavement to power and the negative stagnated and subjected false beliefs formed of ignorance and of ego.

Research Methodology:

This is not so much an academic analysis of a collection of previous works of social theory books, research papers and journal articles. In an attempt to form of their intellectual edifice a new piece of work as a further single individual building block through which to reinforce our already over-justified conceptual arrangements, of deductive schemata, and the generalisations of the logical inferences we base on these foundations. Inferences and generalisations we form in an attempt towards creating a scientific objectivity in our opinions, to try and accurately equate the actual reality and the genuine truth of our individual sociocultural realities, and collective human existence.

It is not a singular testing of the intellectual validity of an individual and newly formed academic concept, through scientifically testing the causation accuracy and truth value of its applied paradigm of pragmatic relevance. A paradigm added to and reinforced through an attempt to realise both the existential 'good faith' (Sartre, 1948), and rational materialist 'justified true belief' (Ayer, 1936), that the social scientist responsible for the concepts creation has placed in the assumed scientific objectivity of the reality of the theoretical concept being schematised or tested. The intention of this manuscript is still absolutely to push the boundary of human intellectual knowledge further than it currently is. To help develop and guide the cutting-edge of the subjects of the greater cultural humanities and the social and political sciences to the new heights of a more refined perspective.

A perspective achieved through the resurrection, realisation, pursuit and actualisation of the potential of new existential realities emerging, made possible through pursuing the belief system of humanism. The reawakening of the cultural meta-narrative ideals of the scientific age of reason and the enlightenment to help develop further the conceptual, experimental and theoretical knowledge of humanity in the expansion of our intellectual, individual, creative and cultural horizons as we push further the boundaries of every human frontier, (Russell, 1938)

It is therefore this manuscripts ambition in its critical analysis and discussion areas to define and elaborate the theoretical perspective of Humanism within the greater socioeconomic context and political and economic frame of reference of the Neo-Modern Research Based Economy (RBE). This is only give light to the symbiotic development of the intellectual culture of science and the parallel of the evolution of our form of society and of our social ideology as correlative factors in the evolution of intellectual culture and how that culture is applied.

Through the rationalistic ideology of humanism and the scientific aspirations of neomodernism, we see the collective interlocking dynamics of a realisable theoretical and practical intellectual duality of political ideology and social policy. An international knit of economic and political interests leading to social and cultural prosperity through the harmonisation of international wealth depolarisation alongside egalitarian democratic power sharing between all countries, will see the flourishing of all left-wing or right-wing realisations of the neomodern humanist ideological blueprint.

Now is the time for the fundamental exposition of a new international political economy, framed within the context of the crumbling and decaying international debt fuelled 'turbo-capitalist' financing of the global world economy. The realisation of the global political ideal placed within the frame of reference of the of the transformation of the real through the research directed international political and economic blueprint.

A blueprint which can be successfully applied by all nations to achieve an economic independence and through it achieve an equality of power sharing between itself and all other countries. Achieved through the collective global technological advancement and the flourishing of all people and societies both individually and as a part of the greater world internationally as a whole.

Then equipped with the inspiration of a new social perspective as the source of fresh political ideology and activism in the social sciences and the subject of the greater academic humanities as a whole might be enough to shake us from the stupor of our stagnated cultural decadence and collective social apathy. Once more within the academic subject of culture our collective human social destiny and the fundamental intellectual concern we have over the fate of the human race could once more have a strong and true undercurrent of rational investigation and ideological inquiry.

In my discussion and conclusion I shall also speculate and explore a number of potential mutually beneficial altruistically aimed global scientific endeavours and international social and cultural objectives for improving the quality of life and lived existential realities for all individuals who suffer from what Hannah Arendt coined famously as 'The Human

22

Condition' of our global civil society, (Arendt, 1958). These ideological social ambitions can then be focused into reality through the successful application of government funding into cultivating newly developing intellectual talent, novel technological ideas and scientific innovations on a local university, national institute and international research committee level of collective aspiration and individual achievement.

Then according to the cultural tenets of Humanism and the ideals of the enlightenment, can we best apply the use of our faculties of intellectual reason and our capacities for creativity, insight and originality to 'the human condition' and continue the development of human culture, science and technology in a way that is truly in agreement with the cultivated 'practical wisdom' that the first Socratic humanists equated with the most perfect and highest state of objective knowledge.

That through following an individual intellectual and creative cultural programme of development as a society and as people we will acquire new knowledge and gain a new level of personal wisdom and introspective understanding through these endeavours. Thus we all benefit from, and never hinder ourselves through the pursuit of enlightenment as the selfish and superficial subjectivities of profit, want, gain, ego, power and motive fade into insignificance in our inspirational and illuminating quest for the true glory of the actual realisation of a brighter future and a better tomorrow.

Critical Analysis:

For more than a decade we the people have accepted the leadership of the ruling elite. We have followed them, blindly, fool heartedly, selfishly in our stupidity pursuing greed, money, power and fame. To the point where we objectify the value of everything which has value with a Dollar or Pound sign. The enslavement of humanity to a symbol, and the symbol of deluded decadence at that.

Virtue, love, wisdom and knowledge may be society's ideals norms and values but all too often they seem sacrificed to the more negative and brutal aspects of our very human nature before it can grow into goodness, and bud. Ultimately this leads us into asking the philosopher's questions like what is a good life? How should we live and treat each other? What is true love? Perhaps to never ask these questions at all is the embodiment of the ignorance of our social epoch; a self fulfilled prophecy of our superficial subjective media influenced minds to become a nothingness of sensual gratification.

Society is a strange beast but beautiful creature as well, to put it in the perspective of the organic analogy. It is a fractal of amalgamated cultural meanings and interactions, revealed by a socially introspective lens of connective will and emotional energies to contemplate and be perceived, an interconnectedness of systematic organic functions spanning all nations, societies and people ultimately connecting all human beings to each other, the environment and out into nature and the greater macro-cosmic natural world.

For too long we have lived under governments

which worship money, wealth and the power it gives them. All just to use their privilege and power to make sure that they're better off than everyone else, because they're in charge, they write the rules, they make the important decisions and they rule, so they believe they should have to pay less tax than everybody else or no tax at all. Wrong.

Then there is us the people, the masses, the general social body which exist to pay more and more taxes. Why? Simple, because it's more money for them to invest in their businesses. This is not a balance of private and public funding, this is robbery, of the people's money, by the kleptocratic minority that we allow to rule over us.

The time has come for change but change without a plan is chaos and if we are to evolve and refine society then setting ablaze to a current one as probably not a good idea. So I present two perspectives here, one left wing, and one right wing, the degree to which they are both applied in turn defines our place in the political or socioeconomic spectrum of ourselves and our society. Liberty or liberalism is the glue which bonds both together and allows us to be midway between the two and embody some aspects of either side of the political polemic. It is freedom of choice to choose our political perspective with our freedom of speech to criticize those in power, our politicians, if they are failing us much like they currently are.

So what I call for is not social Revolution but social evolution where the global powers interests all interlock instead of conflict and individuals live inspired and free, in a social creature of meaning, will and intentionality. Interconnected through all aspects of meaning in our ever-growing capacity to engender autonomy in our will and freedom, hope and love in our hearts. This section is about something I've called the research directed economy, it details exactly how to advance the current level of technology and science that society has available to it creating and maintaining a valid export market, booming industrial sector and thriving job market. It is an ideological policy solution for the vast majority of problems that society suffers from. The best way to put it, is it is the social policy and ideology of the future. So with no hesitation, here it is:

If you use the social structure and social institution of higher education as the base of operations for research into new technologies and new avenues of science which seeks to advance humanity and grant us freedom from the chains of bondage born of ignorance which one's restrained us then essentially speaking you have operationalised the most important social structure that exists in the social body. In Parsons organic analogy you could like them the government to the brain of society. But I would liken the current government to the most basic survival driven parts of the brain and the neocortex, the more advanced areas would be our further and higher education. It contains our capacity for social advancement through the enlightenment which knowledge brings, higher education is not just our capacity for logic and reason it is our capacity for meaning, culture and creation as well.

Now the first question you are going to ask is this; this is all well and good but where are we going with this? How are we going to afford to pay for the advancement of our social structure. My answer is this: the Kleptocrats. Now I have nothing against anybody who tries to make their own wealth becoming a self-employed business owner, but when your business is untaxed in years and responsible for hoarding hundreds of billions of pounds on non-invested capital at the expense of the wealth, quality of life and prosperity of the greater 99% in high interest accounts with the banks generating money for the sake of having money leads to money making money simply through it's very existence. Hence the rich become even richer, the poor even poorer and the polemic of wealth and poverty stretches to even more extreme ends than they were to begin with, with no positive social mobility in sight.

So I put it like this if you want a fair social system with all the operating social structures and institutions funded properly then you do not have to make the poor pay for it, they are poor, they have no money, an underclass of poverty, people for which there is no work. So instead of granting tax breaks to a richest one percent of society at the expensive of the quality of life of the other ninety-nine percent, grant tax breaks to the poorest ninety-nine percent and tax the hell out the richest, that have little concept of the true value of things nor the wisdom necessary to earn the reverence they currently receive. But this is robbery you say, it's against our human rights, it's against the social systems values? No, no it isn't, it is redistribution of excess capital from the bourgeois elite through tax to the proletarian wage slave majority.

Don't get me wrong I'm not after your hard-earned cash, I don't want to rob you of your earnings and should you get wealthy I certainly don't want to infringe upon the quality of your life when you enjoy your money. What I am against is the hoarding of hundreds and thousands of billions of pounds which essentially have been earned through undercutting with the little guy in the mass exploitation of every worker in society. We work to pay for the luxuries of our employers and the exclusive ultra-rich elite, and thus the further the two extremes of the polemic of wealth and poverty are pushed as we pay for the luxury, opulence and privilege of the the upper-classes and guess what this super elite runs your society.

But I'm very aware of the direction of this book is geared is towards social evolution not social revolution. There is no intention of juxtaposing the leaders of our society, who may or may not be tyrants, with new leaders, who also may or may not turn out to be tyrants themselves. So considering this I propose the following; the only way to change society is to put a deal on the table which literally benefits everybody, from the most impoverished, to the most wealthy. If it is something that benefits everybody, and is agreeable to the norms and values of our society and culture, then why not make it so.

So what I propose is this: Scrap all personal income tax, from the top of society and the most elite, to bottom of the pile and the people living on the streets. The consequence of this shift in socioeconomic policy is that everybody in society has more money to spend, everybody is better off. To counterbalance this lost tax revenue for the government, you tax the hell out of the profits of the non-reinvested accumulated capital of multinational big business, and pour that money back into society, into upwards class mobility and the public social institutions like education and the National Health Service. If we are truly democratic and believe in equality, liberty and meritocracy, then truly there should be no unfair advantages or disadvantages to our opportunities and chosen destiny. But with policy of this nature in place everybody gets a fair deal and an increased and better quality of life: through having

28

more money. So there we have it! This is where the funding comes from, that is where the money is coming from, to pay for the advancement of society and for collective social progressive change, I shall now to describe in detail the research based economy:

Higher education is where you have all the academics and intellectually and creatively minded people. The cutting-edge thinkers, wise philosophers, keenest scientists and the cultural leaders of our societies day and age. These are the people in whom it is invested to bring up, teach and train the next generation of the leaders of our society. They are intellectually, creatively and scientifically speaking the very best we have. So as we can see, the natural talent already in education acts a concentrated hub, an epicentre of advanced thinking and technological development. It is research of these higher education institutions that paves the way for the future of human understanding, science and technology, not funded on the basis of its profitability or cash value. Technology it is funded on the basis of its unique potential to advance the human race, and better the human condition. It is just this sort of egalitarian thinking that needs to be emphasised in the chronic anti-empathic culture of segregated isolated individuals who are embittered through their failings who curse the positive tenets of liberty, freedom of speech and future social ideology before it can even take root in the fertile soils of humanities infinite untapped potential.

In higher education you have all the master's degree holders and all the post-honours holders and the vast majority of the professors that our society has. You have a concentration of intellectual and creative genius already working at the cutting edge of science, technology and culture, all we do now is much like I hope for the NHS that they see the solutions it provides and give it the funding it deserves.

Just to reiterate one more time; the money to fund this research and social advancement is not coming out of your hard-earned cash it is not coming out your tax it is coming out of accumulated uninvested stale decadent profit of the richest of the elite in society, who for some unknown reason we provide tax breaks to, whilst the poor pay in the milking of the masses, this is grossly unfair and needs to change, and will. So with all the tax from the hyper-rich elite put into research and development of new technologies at institutions of higher education, then as a scientist once said for every $1 we put into space program we got fifteen dollars back, this wealth multiplication situation through technological advancement still exists, and should, unlike the workers be the only thing exploited by society. So with all our new found funding donated by the generosity and philanthropy of the rich, or just taken from them, perhaps the government should engender this positive economic activity so surely it should stop the senseless accumulation and hoarding of wealth by the elite for the sake of their own power and no other higher legitimate reason.

The concentration of the intellectual and cultural genius of our society are put to a best effort, they have the capacity to create the most positive change that they can, and will. So with this massive investment in research and development into new sciences and new technologies all of the graduate and postgraduate degree holders are enticed back to their universities to become full time research staff. The best thing about this is that these research post holders could have it written into their contracts that they teach so many hours a week to undergraduates, basically meaning that undergraduates can go to university for free, because the funding is paid for out of research budgets not their personal pocket. Now let me explain what you do do once you have researched and developed these technologies.

Well because our nation is now producing high technology goods that cannot be mass produced elsewhere in other countries cheaper, undercutting the value and sovereignty of our exports market, through marginal income accumulation, where we are out competed by the rest of the world. So when considering a purchase do you buy better or cheaper? Ultimately the quality of cheaper becomes better and better and that's when you're screwed, because that means you haven't got any viable goods or services to sell the rest of the world. It's a bit like a shopkeeper selling goods, only the shop is society, but the shops got no goods in it that anybody desires because they can buy the same goods or services elsewhere cheaper.

So guess what mate, you are flogging a dead horse! you haven't got a viable business if you have no niche market of consumers and no viable products in the first place. If you are going to run the country like a business, then at least run it at a profit and not a loss. Yet with the research economy new technological goods are produced by the considered country that cannot be mass produced, elsewhere, cheaper. So with the high technology market saturated with new and novel high technology goods we have once more a viable export market. Yes, that means that the country is making money for a change instead of stockpiling the national debt deficit as a source of funding (which under the Conservative Party has doubled!).

Economic prosperity is founded on the the

grounds that we have money coming into this country from other countries, increasing our wealth and prosperity tenfold. It also entices and attracts many graduates and postgraduates back into the higher education system to become researchers and teachers. This also contributes positively to the availability of work in the national job market because the more high skilled jobs there are, the less high skilled workers you have occupying low skilled jobs so there are more high skill jobs and more low skill jobs as a consequence.

But here's the best bit once you have researched new avenues of science and the new technologies this researched knowledge brings not only does it open up the potential for the flourishing of the human race, but also has a valid socioeconomic impact on the distribution and polarisation of wealth in society as well. With these new technologies established as public ownership patents there are two things which can be done, either individually or both together.

The first thing you can do is very similar to what happens already apart from it's much less corrupt version of the preferential government backed private business funding which happens already. Namely you can either stimulate the industrial sector with production rights contract for the most ethical and sound industry competitors, which also constitutes as a part of the cash return on the investments of the people an industry competitor down-payment for the production rights, further supplemented by monthly payments to the government out of the profit that these new technologies bri9ng, causing an immediate return on the investment the government has made in higher education, science and technology.

The other slightly more radical option is this; if

the government sets up proxy businesses to sell these new high technology goods and services to the people of the nation at a significantly reduced cost for the government holds the production rights in the form of public ownership patents. So instead of selling off the production rights to the industrial sector, the government undercuts the profit margins of industry leaders through out researching their level of technological and scientific development, setting up proxy businesses to out compete the financial competition. Therefore through undercutting big business more money goes to public hands then goes to big business and private ultra-rich elitist hands.

So there you have it, the intrinsic dynamics of the high technology market guarantees the national success of the high technology product, which is run on behalf of the people by the government as an agent of economic investment for the people, on behalf of the people. Producing high technology at a fraction of its true value and cost leading to a thriving internal national market and demand for these goods of high technology as well as guaranteeing the success and profitability of the export market through their novelty, practicality and originality.

The economic consequence of this social structure in action is basically that money is taken out of the greedy hoarding clutches of private and political financial investors and placed in the hands of the public purse. In other words under this new taxation strategy the people, all people, in society have more money in their personal pockets across the boarder spectrum of society and big business with their excessive reserve wealth basically has less. The research economy is essentially a creatable social structure in post-modern society which redistributes money and wealth from the richest one percent of societies members to the other ninety-nine percent of the wage-slave working proletariat who deserve this money in their pocket as for whom this monetary increase through no income tax would make a real and significant legitimate difference to their quality of life.

So there we have it, in a nutshell, the ideological foundation to the basis of the research economy; that through higher education research funding we can revive the export market, stimulate the industrial sector and create a new viable income for the nation through the sale of high technology, that cannot be mass produced elsewhere by other countries at a significantly cheaper price. This becomes a future globally inclusive ideology when all countries of the world catch on and start researching different technologies in different research directions and down different avenues, creating an internationally sound and viable export market for each and every nation to sell their high technology goods to each and every other nation and create a balance of wealth and prosperity on the global level henceforth. When all Nations and developed countries adopt this social strategy of research based prosperity and fecundity then we will see the progressive interlocking of international research agendas around the world, creating for each nation a viable export market so that no society or individual should be forced to live a poor quality of life or struggle in poverty.

Discussion:

As the neomodern research economy can be applied and adapted to nearly all different types of social and political structures and systems, there really is so much potential for variation and also success among different national realisations of the research based economy when it is considered on the international level.

The success of those seeking employment without realising it depends largely upon the success and growth of the graduate job market. This is because influences at a fundamental level, the overpricing and undergraduate 'tuition fee' funded nature of the current higher education system in Great Britain prices out most people from going into higher education and actualising their ambitions and achieving their dreams, (Maslow, 1943).

But not just the educational prosperity of individual success through achieving their level of qualification is effected by the exclusivity of the qualification. But also the greater effects that shrinkage of the graduate job market has upon the success, growth and prosperity of the job market for individuals employed in other areas at different levels as well is effected.

This is because if there is a lack of graduate employment prospects, then graduates are forced into lesser educated job roles and employment, not only saturating the graduate job market but taking away jobs which would rightfully be filled by other people though not as highly qualified, but just as capable of filling the employment position, saturating the job market at other levels.

The end result is the socioeconomic stagnation

of the employment system, where there is a severe lack of meaningful work for all but the most highly qualified elite people in society. This increases as you go down the social strata, meaning for the lowest income workers, there is the lowest job security or chance of the availability of decent paid employment.

The development of the higher education social structure into the research sector who develop public owned patents gives businesses competing for production rights more incentive to develop their own research programs as well in order to keep up with current latest developments and levels of technological advancement within the different areas in which his businesses operate and greater society as a whole.

With the growth of the export market industry desires for more designers and producers of innovative new technologies and scientific discoveries, in order to keep pace with the national research initiative and development of public owned patent This means the graduate job market grows immensely, offering not just employment for new graduates, but also employment opportunities for the massive number of graduates currently employed in less specialised and educated job roles. Graduates who can now either return to higher education and further learning or acquire employment to the level of which they have been trained.

Also because the most specialised and educated leaders in field and associated professors and doctors will be at the different nationally and internationally public patent funded universities to do research. So if you include written into the returning graduates contract that they have to teach a few undergraduate students as well, then therefore with such a high concentration of talent and specialist geniuses the undergraduate students get the best level of education and can go to collage or university for free.

So with the flourishing of national research based economies we should see on the national level the redistribution of wealth from the richest top one percent in society who hold ninety five percent of the wealth, to the poorer ninety-nine percent of people who have significantly less than one percent of societies wealth. This comes in the form of profit paid from the state to individual from the export sales of new high technologies to other nations and distribution retailers who wish to supply these nations intrinsic demand for high technology goods and services.

The production rights of these high technology products whether it be from the businesses who are contracted for mass reproduction contracts or through companies set up specifically by the government to represent the public owned patents of the people the potential for success in a Neo-Modern global market is remarkable. As for the global level of research we see a knitting of the worlds technological interests divided between individual Nations as national research projects and global research projects which then give each nation specialised technology developments. Which are desired by all other Nations and unique applications them without establishing a monopoly or global power centralisation within the free market and the sociopolitical spectrum of international economic power and wealth. Thus leading to the prosperity of all Nations and the flourishing of all societies and individuals within those societies across the globe.

The question as to whether the humanist ideal of social progress can be achieved in our lifetimes really depends upon what we ourselves intend to achieve in our lifetimes. The originally Marxist theory of historical materialism is that to all societies there is a fixed and set socioeconomic and political end state to which all social systems evolution and future is destined.

This is based upon the cyclic predictability of a human individuals behaviours, the cultural dynamics of ideological explanation and the understanding which we adhere to in our interpretation of the greater world. The intellectual validity of what Marx & Engels saw as the scientific laws of socioeconomic evolution of which the collective end state of liberal democratic socialism is the final ideal society, or utopia.

But unlike the predictions of Engels & Marx of the progressive establishment of a new legitimated economic and political power, through suffering the exploitation of social inequalities by those with this power, would cause rebellion. The collective cultural realisation of the power struggle inherent within society and its final conclusion of the inevitable revolution of the exploited majority or proletariat against the oppressive wealthy minority or bourgeoisie to try establish socialism and true equality fell desperately short of their hopes and expectations.

Their own ethnocentrism was borne of the enlightenment and industrial capitalist eras individualist belief in the democratic freedom and the political equality of all members of society. An equality established with the ideal of humanist freedoms and the value of human rights and our own personal liberty and freedom which was established by capitalism replacing feudalism.

Unfortunately they did not enshrine liberty in their own ideology, in the ideals of their socialist political doctrine deeply enough for it to be embodied in the Socialist societies which did come to pass.

Countries who failed to see it's true value and often labelled it as the ideological illusion of a dominant global capitalist order which still in its cultural propaganda calls itself liberal democracy.

The humanist and Marxist philosophical school of thought will be quick to legitimise their cultural objectivity by highlighting that the sociocultural laws of evolution and the individual dynamics of personal causation determine the manifestation of our collective social destiny. But predictions according to those laws are entirely dependent upon the development of our own personal autonomy, and our capacity for social action which is within the intellectual scope of the liberal democratic freedoms we have.

A liberty which is necessary for the cultural idealism of socialism to be fully realised and achieved by the Proletariat and not sidelined by the despotic authoritarianism of a new elite sensing the completion of social change and the gratification of their own personal superficial visceral desire for power and personal glory.

In order for a truly emancipating, empowering and liberating collective identity or state of shared cultural consciousness to emerge within the thoughts, attitudes and minds of the individual people within a particular generational period. It is essential that we engage in acts which make us more informed and educated as to the realities of social inequality and personal suffering in the world in order to increase our personal autonomy, capacity to make decisions and ultimately act. To help bring about the destiny which will embody the ideals we hold truest, the two most fundamental concerning how we treat ourselves and each other being power and love.

The two fundamental existential concepts which

govern the essential nature which we manifest within our own existence as the energies of our self orientation and empathic alignment towards others are power & love.

Of these he polar opposites of the authoritarian and egalitarian personality are formed; the former a self idolising and empathising individual who seeks control and dominion over others, the later a socially empathic and caring person who seeks insight and control over their own self and mind. One, an agent of world war; the other, an agent of world peace.

The nature of our conscious mind being the apex of focus for the subconscious processes and dynamics which determines the nature of our thoughts. As our thoughts arise as the fixations of the unconscious mind, which naturally seeks to express and bring to fruition the desires of the intelligence and intellect of the individual. It can be said that the power of thoughts, and collective belief, has the true capacity to influence and change reality.

This being said, if we believe within our thoughts in the ideal of social progress and will for its manifestation as a universal deontological law, and as a cultural group and part of society we collectively believe in social progress as a valued ideal, (Kant, 1788; Kant; 1790). Then social progress will as a consequence naturally harmonise through the empathic resonances of the social subconscious and with ease come to manifest in both cultural attitudes and social actions, (Jung, 1991)..

A research based economy appears to be the perfect instigator and agent for increasing individual autonomy and generating positive social advancement in the future of our collective tangent of social human destiny. The creation of public owned patents and the social ownership of technology production rights leads to growth of the export market and this leads to huge increases in both social revenue and private profit earned. The money earned from it will ensure that for every nation involved their export market will definitely provide the best source of both the economic prosperity and innovative technological strength of a nation.

This is because these new innovative technologies developed by graduates in a neo-modern technologies market of research based economies, leads to even more innovative and unique goods and services being designed and developed. Created outside of the education based research sector increasing the level of scientific and technological advancement of a nation and of the whole human race even more.

This is because each nation produces uniquely specialised technology which in turn cannot be over produced in other more industrialised countries cheaper through the mass production capacities of the technologies industry who flood the market. This means these high technology products have economic validity in an international market and will definitely lead to the economic success and individual flourishing of all nations who employ the neo-modern research sector economic strategy.

The money gained from the export market profits, sales and production rights contracts should eventually replace tax as the primary source of income for the funding of the social system and state apparatus. Through redistributing wealth from private profit to national public ownership of capital produced by the neo-modern research sector economy this will contribute greatly to wealth depolarisation, universal human prosperity and the flourishing of all individuals across the planet.

The ideals of humanism are very much alive at the heart of the Neo-Modern agenda, the combination of the two ideological perspectives really could constitute to a truly world changing and paradigm shifting global perspective for the future of the humanity. A social perspective which is the embodiment of the empowerment and cooperation of individuals as opposed to human race which was the embodiment of aggression, violence, competition and unfair 'war of all against all', (Hobbes, 1651).

Conclusion:

Hopefully if all countries can evolve their interpretation of the existential truths and facts that dictate and determine the nature of human lived reality, then the international social system and ideological structuring of human social reality can evolve further to an even greater beauty then we are capable of envisioning in our highest and greatest ideals and dreams for the realisation of our greatest potential as individuals and cultural beings.

Then considering the nature of interaction of nations and countries with other nations and countries will of evolved to a level of cooperation and empathetic existential compassion so that the culture of violence and aggressive competition which appears to be the social, cultural, intellectual, individual and internationally embodied acceptable norm for our day and age will of finally become obsolete and ceased to be an acceptable standard of social and political human interaction.

We will have emerged into a golden era of world peace instead of slipping into another era of world war. Where we all are victims and we are forced on a individual, social and political state level into a prolonged period of unnecessary violence, destruction and the dark chaos of inhumane suffering, abuse and sickening war crimes the brutality of which we can never speak the actual horror of.

I hope we emerge into another era of the greater collective social culture of acceptable interaction based on cooperation and compassion instead of the current one of avarice and competition. Where on a international and individual level this unacceptable culture will cease to be as an acceptable ideology of human interaction.

But this will only come to be if I was standards of cultural interaction on a international and a individual level have actualised their capacity to evolve. Through having had the right conditions to enable the potential of human social culture to evolve these ethical and cultural capacities of our true inner higher nature to come to manifest.

This positive future will only come to pass if we have evolved our culture of acceptable social and political interaction from one of aggression and competition to one compassion and cooperation on both international, social, cultural and individual level of human interaction and acceptable collective behaviour.

As all disease and illness manifests and works through either exhibiting causation upon a mechanism of action or causing a mechanism of action in its own right to influence further causal systems and have its manifest properties as the symptoms of an illness. Then by definition of the limits, boundaries of and nature of its causation all illness and disease can essentially be prevented or cured by the capacity and capabilities of the correct application of the constantly developing and evolving nature of scientific endeavour, technological advancement and developed medical practice.

Therefore through understanding the mechanisms of action of a disease we can counter influence this mechanism of action by effecting a dynamic of influence upon the system of its causation. One which allows the disease or illness to have its effect upon the body and manifest it's undesirable symptoms upon a human individual.

`All disease and illness has its fundamental

properties of biological and chemical causation and its manifest physical symptoms. So then essentially through counteracting the origin of the effects of the causation of an illness, which is producing manifest symptoms, through medical intervention; then we have the potential to eventually to eradicate all illness and disease from human existence.

The task may appear to be a daunting one but once we realise our true potential and collective capacities as human individuals, collective identities and the greater human society and civilization of humanity as a whole then such a task can actually realistically be solved. As one of human races main problems is its issue with limited and depleting resources from which to sustain it's it's existence in terms of water, food and materials of practical value then we need a plan or stratagem of how to deal with this need and cope with the ever changing demands of the global natural and human environment.

Essentially in the name of humanism we must apply science and Neo-Modernism and develop technologies to adapt to the crisis which human race suffers from in its fundamental nature and as a species and society has always suffered together. This is because we consume resources and because this produces waste. Reason and logical practical thought must supply the science and technology in form of recycling used resources from the waste which we produce.

We must also enable the shifting of energy production from the limited depleting resources of the petroleum industry as a fundamental supplier of energy to renewable sources in order for humanity to be able to sustain itself into the future. So hopefully with the idealism of humanism and neo modernism we can develop further the mode of production toward the energy production based mechanised we will be able to supply the demands for energy indefinitely perhaps even infinitely.

Once the human race has evolved a culture of cooperation and not competition on a international level then hopefully we will be unified enough to seriously consider space colonization on a interplanetary level and travel to other star systems be a serious possibility in the near future. Once we are evolved enough to be able to realise the potential for interstellar travel and civilization and have not succumb to another world war through the culture of violence and war which will ultimately without humanity taking control of its destiny destroy us all through weapons of mass destruction.

Through the inability to effectively deal through cooperation on an international level with the threat of a cosmic world ending event because we have devolved to such a level where ultimately we are left helpless and live under medieval despots as victims with the human race completing a cycle of life by destroying itself through its inability to deal with a fundamental crisis. As a social species we must overcome the issues which our species faces in political and economic and ecological reality and are capable of realising the existential truth of our human situation and its conditions upon us as individuals and a species.

I hope only the human race evolves to this level of cooperation and empathetic existential compassion and does not destroy itself in another world war of all against all in which human race destroys itself abandoning the ideals it is tried so long to achieve as cultural fact and political science. So now we have a blueprint for human social and cultural evolution and the prospects of new scientific breakthroughs and advances on our doorstep.

Let us hope that we take our potential and transform it into our reality, turning the ideals we have embodied and loved all our lives in to the realities of the future generations. I wish the most positive future possible for humanity as our capacities are limited only by our beliefs and in order to create change the world we must first have envisioned our capacity to create it in our lifetimes.

Bibliography:

Adorno, T., (2001) Culture Industry: Selected Essays on Mass Culture, Routledge: London.

Arendt, H., (1958) The Human Condition, University of Chicago Press: Chicago.

Aristotle, (2002) Ethics, Penguin Classics: London.

Ayer, A.J. (1936) Language, Truth & Logic, Dover: New York.

Becker, H., (1963) Outsiders, Free Press: New York.

Bourdieu, P., (1977) Outline of a Theory of Practice, Cambridge University Press: London.

Cohen, S., (1972) Folk Devils & Moral Panics: The Creation of The Mods & Rockers, Routledge Classics: London.

Comte, A., (1865) A General View Of Positivism, Franklin Classics: New York.

Dawkins, R., (1976) The Selfish Gene, Oxford University Press: Oxford.

Durkheim, E., The Division of Labour In Society: The Free Press: New York.

Garfoot, A.P., (2010) Dawn of The Neo-Modern: Art, Humanism & The Meme, Lulu Press: London.

Garfoot, A.P. (2012) Faster Than Light Travel & How To Destroy A Dwarf Star, Lulu Press: London.

Gramsci, A., (2005) Selections from the Prison Notebooks of Antonio Gramsci, Lawrence & Wishart Ltd.: London.

Hobbes, T., (1651) The Leviathan, Cambridge University Press: Cambridge.

Hume, D., ((1740) A Treatise Of Human Nature, Penguin Classics: London.

Hume, D., (1748) Enquiries Concerning Human Understanding, Penguin: London.

Jung, C.G., (1991)The Archetypes and the Collective Unconscious, Routledge: London.

Kant, I., (1788) Critique Of Practical Reason, Penguin: London

Kant, I., (1790) Critique Of Judgement, Penguin Classics: London.

Kuhn, T., (1962) The Structure Of Scientific Revolutions, University Of Chicago Press.

Lyotard, J.J., (1984) The Postmodern Condition, University of Minnesota Press: Minneapolis.

Marx, K., & Engels, F., (1832) The German Ideology, Hackett: Indianapolis.

Marx, K., & Engels, F., (1848) The Communist Manifesto, Penguin Classics: London.

Maslow, A.H., (1943) "A Theory of Human Motivation" In Psychological Review, 50, (4), 430-437.

Mead, G.H., (1967) Mind, Self & Society, University of Chicago Press: Chicago.

Merton, R.K, (1968) Social Theory and Social Structure, Free Press: New York.

Mill, J.S., (1859) On Liberty, Simon & Schuster: London.

Nietzsche F., (1886) Beyond Good & Evil, Penguin Classics: London.

Parsons, T., (1951) The Social System, Free Press: Glencoe.

Pavlov, I., (1927) Conditioned Reflexes, Dover: London.

Popper, K., (1952) The Open Society & Its Enemies, Princeton University Press: New York.

Russell, B., (1938) Power: A New Social Analysis, Allen & Unwin: London.

Sartre, J.P., (1948) Existentialism & Humanism, Ken Jackson: London.

Skinner, B.F. (1938) The Behaviour of Organisms: An

Experimental Analysis, Appleton-Century-Crofts: East Norwalk.

Weber, M., (1905) The Protestant Ethic and The Spirit of Capitalism, Penguin Classics: London.

Willis, P., (1977) Learning To Labour, Columbia University Press: New York.

www.ingramcontent.com/pod-product-compliance
Lightning Source LLC
Chambersburg PA
CBHW070130290526
45789CB00005B/2188